Zumpango

Tizayuca

Xaltocan

Teotihuacan

Cuautitlán

Tepexpan

Ecatepec

Acolman

Azcapotzalco

Tlacopan
(Tacuba)

Tlatelolco

Tezcoco

Tenochtitlan

Chapultepec

Coyoacán

Culhuacán

Cuitláhuac

Chalco

Xochimilco

Chimalpan

The Poet King of Tezcoco

Even though the codices and monuments created by the peoples of the valley of Mexico were destroyed in the Spanish Conquest, we know about Nezahualcóyotl's life because several native historians decided to preserve his memory. Most important was a direct descendant named Fernando de Alva Ixtlilxóchitl. In the early seventeenth century, he devoted himself to gathering manuscripts and information about the pre-Conquest period in Mexico and wrote *Historia de la nación chichimeca* [History of the Chichimec Nation]. The main part of the book is a biography of Nezahualcóyotl. Alva Ixtlilxóchitl also collected many of Nezahualcóyotl's poems and translated them from Nahuatl to Spanish. The sixteenth-century historian Juan Bautista Pomar, a descendant of Nezahualpilli's mother's family, wrote *Relación de Tezcoco* [The Story of Tezcoco], which provides many useful facts about life in Tezcoco. Pomar's book and the writings of Alva Ixtlilxóchitl are the most reliable sources of information about the history of Tezcoco. Another valuable document is the *Códice Xólotl* [Xólotl Codex], a post-Conquest copy of a codex written in the court of Tezcoco during the fifteenth century—that is, during Nezahualcóyotl's era or not long after—which provides vivid descriptions of episodes in Nezahualcóyotl's life. In modern times, the historians Ángel María Garibay and Miguel León-Portilla have translated Nezahualcóyotl's poems from Nahuatl to Spanish, and José Luis Martínez has published a biography of Nezahualcóyotl that brings together most of the information preserved about him.

The Poet King of Tezcoco  A Great Leader of Ancient Mexico

By Francisco Serrano

Illustrated by Pablo Serrano

*Biography translated
and adapted by* Trudy Balch

*Poetry translated
by* Jo Anne Engelbert

Groundwood Books
House of Anansi Press
Toronto   Berkeley

His Birth and the Tribulations of His Youth

I WILL CREATE A WORK OF ART

I will create a work of art.
I am a poet, and my song
will endure on earth.
I will be remembered for my songs.

The sun was just beginning to rise on the morning of April 28, 1402, known in the Aztec calendar as "day 1 Deer of the year 1 Rabbit," when Prince Acolmiztli Nezahualcóyotl was born in the city of Tezcoco, capital of the kingdom of Tezcoco. His name came from two Nahuatl words that mean "lion's strength" and "fasting coyote." Astrologers predicted that the boy would be astute, proud, nimble and strong, just like his sign, the deer. But he would have to be vigilant and flee to escape his enemies.

Ixtlilxóchitl

Matlacihuatzin

Acolmiztli
Nezahualcóyotl

Nezahualcóyotl was six years old when his parents sent him to the *tlacateo*, a school where he began to receive the strict education traditional for the nobility. He learned to read and write, and he also learned about the ancient and refined culture of his Toltec ancestors. When he turned twelve, a solemn ceremony was held in which he stood next to his father, King Ixtlilxóchitl, and took his oath as crown prince of the kingdom of Tezcoco.

The tlacateo was the school for the nobility.

By the time Nezahualcóyotl reached his sixteenth birthday, his father was in the midst of fighting a war against the nearby kingdom of Azcapotzalco, ruled by the Tepanec leader Tezozómoc. One day, after a harsh battle, King Ixtlilxóchitl was ambushed by a group of Tezozómoc's henchmen. Helpless, Prince Nezahualcóyotl hid in a treetop and watched as his father died from the attackers' blows. At dawn the next day, a faithful vassal helped Nezahualcóyotl retrieve his father's body and cremate it, in accordance with Toltec funeral tradition. This was the beginning of many misfortunes, persecutions and perils.

Nezahualcóyotl's father is killed.

The Fugitive Prince

THAT I MIGHT NEVER DIE

I am confounded.
I worry, I think, I wish
that I might never die,
that I might never disappear!

That I might reach the realm
where death does not exist,
where death is overcome.

If I might never die,
if I might never disappear!

When Tezozómoc learned of Ixtlilxóchitl's death, he rewarded the killers and proclaimed himself king of Tezcoco. He was determined to wipe out all memory of the rightful king, whose death he had ordered. Even more, he wanted to prevent Nezahualcóyotl from taking Tezcoco back. Tezozómoc offered prizes and rewards to anyone who would bring Nezahualcóyotl to him, dead or alive, and he swore he would punish anyone who offered the young prince any help. Several of Nezahualcóyotl's vassals hid him anyway, and then they snuck him into the court of Tenochtitlan, on an island in Lake Tezcoco. The king there was his uncle, Chimalpopoca, the third *tlatoani*, or ruler, of the Aztecs.

Tezozómoc's messenger

Nezahualcóyotl was happy to be near some of his family, but he knew it was too dangerous to stay in one place. He went from one neighboring kingdom to another, traveling by day and keeping a close watch by night. Patient, shrewd and cunning, he was getting ready to take back his kingdom.

For a time, he took refuge in Tlaxcala, to the southeast. Then he disguised himself as a soldier and traveled to Chalco. But when he asked a woman there for something to drink, she recognized him and began to scream. With nowhere to turn, Nezahualcóyotl began to hit her with his club so that his enemies wouldn't catch him. But they captured him anyway, locked him up and condemned him to death.

A nobleman called Quetzalmacatzin took pity on him, and when the soldiers came to put Nezahualcóyotl to death, Quetzalmacatzin released him and helped him flee. Then he put on Nezahualcóyotl's clothes and took his place, and the soldiers killed him instead. Nezahualcóyotl managed to find a place to hide and later returned to Tlaxcala.

After that, his mother's sisters persuaded Tezozómoc to pardon him on the condition that he go back to Tenochtitlan and stay there. And so, despite the threats still

Nezahualcóyotl in captivity

hanging over him, Nezahualcóyotl lived peacefully in the Aztec capital for six years, from 1420 to 1426. He finished his education and his military training, and he probably wrote his first poems.

But he never stopped preparing to overthrow Tezozómoc, who broke his promises to Nezahualcóyotl's aunts and kept trying to crush him.

One night Tezozómoc had a dream that filled him with anguish. He dreamed that Nezahualcóyotl had turned into an eagle, and that the eagle was tearing open his chest and eating his heart.

The next night he dreamed that Nezahualcóyotl had turned into a jaguar, and that the jaguar was biting him all over and devouring his feet. Terrified, Tezozómoc sent for his three sons and told them his dreams.

"We must kill Nezahualcóyotl," they decided. "We must stop him from getting Tezcoco once and for all."

In March of 1427, Tezozómoc died. He had named his son Tayatzin to succeed him, but Maxtla, the oldest, soon forced Tayatzin from the throne. Maxtla was cruel and ambitious, and he began to attack other kingdoms nearby. He captured the Aztec king Chimalpopoca and locked him away.

Even though it was dangerous, Nezahualcóyotl went to Azcapotzalco to plead for his uncle's freedom. Maxtla pretended to let Chimalpopoca go and then tried to kill Nezahualcóyotl, but Nezahualcóyotl managed to escape. To get even, Maxtla ordered Chimalpopoca to be put to death, but the old king hanged himself first.

Tezozómoc's dream

Maxtla's soldiers kept trying to catch Nezahualcóyotl, but he always got away. Once, Maxtla sent the bravest captains in his army after him when he was hiding in the palaces at Cillan, on the eastern shore of Lake Tezcoco.

"Hand him over," Maxtla's captains told Nezahualcóyotl's faithful servant, Coyohua, pointing their spears at him. Instead, Coyohua led them into an enormous room. Suddenly Nezahualcóyotl appeared and offered them bouquets of flowers. Maxtla's men were confused. What should they do now? Then Coyohua ordered the other servants to stir up the braziers of copal incense in the center of the room. As thick clouds of smoke began to rise, he quickly spread his cloak to hide Nezahualcóyotl, who escaped through a hole that had been dug for him behind the throne. When the smoke finally cleared, Maxtla's soldiers realized that the cunning prince had eluded them once again.

Furious, Maxtla ordered the soldiers to pursue Nezahualcóyotl without mercy. But many other people wanted to help the young prince. They despised Maxtla, just as they had hated his tyrannical father, Tezozómoc. Nezahualcóyotl succeeded in uniting many kingdoms around his cause. He formed an alliance with the new king of Tenochtitlan, Izcóatl (who was also his uncle), and then the two of them joined together with the king of Tacuba, forming the Triple Alliance. Backed by a vast army, they attacked Maxtla's troops, chased them away, and took everything they could from Azcapotzalco. It is said that Nezahualcóyotl himself took Maxtla's life. He was twenty-five years old.

His Rise to the Throne

MOST PRECIOUS FLOWERS

*We adorn ourselves
with flowers and with songs,
the loveliness of spring,
growing rich with flowers
here on earth!*

After his triumph over Maxtla, Nezahualcóyotl lived in Tenochtitlan, where he built roads, canals and bridges. Four years later, at the age of twenty-nine, he took the throne of Tezcoco and began to rebuild the kingdom, which had fallen into ruin under Maxtla and Tezozómoc. To help revive Tezcoco's cities, Nezahualcóyotl built palaces and houses for the nobles of his court, each according to their status and merit.

*Nezahualcóyotl
is declared king of Tezcoco.*

Nezahualcóyotl divided the city of Tezcoco into six municipal districts, and grouped the people of each district into neighborhoods that were organized by trade. The goldsmiths and silversmiths lived in one part, the feather artists in another, and all the other trades in separate neighborhoods too.

Next Nezahualcóyotl set up a
new legal system. He established a
strict code of eighty laws, divided
into four sections, with a
supreme council responsible for each one.

The first council heard civil and
criminal cases, and when someone was found guilty, severe punishment followed.
Traitors to the king, for example, were cut into pieces. Their houses were sacked and
torn down, the land underneath was sown with salt, and their children and other
relatives became slaves for the next four generations. Princes or nobles who rebelled
against their lords met the same fate, and so did anyone who wore the king's insignias
or emblems without permission, even the crown prince himself. This tribunal also dealt
with matters concerning slaves, with lawsuits and disputes over land, property and
goods, and with disagreements involving the various trades.

The second council was for
music and the sciences. It tried
and punished crimes and
superstitious acts committed by
witches and sorcerers.

Only necromancy—predicting the future by trying to communicate with the dead—was permitted, because it did not harm anyone.

The third council was the war council, which judged military issues. Soldiers who did not follow their captain's orders or did not carry out their duties were beheaded. If they robbed or wrongfully took anything from a captive or from war booty, they were hanged. Soldiers and captains in the king's guard were hanged if the king went to war and was captured by his enemies. The guards' duty was to see that the king returned, dead or alive.

Finally, there was the treasury council, whose judges supervised the collection and distribution of tribute, a kind of tax system in which wealth was paid to the king. Tribute collectors who took in more than vassals and subjects were supposed to pay were condemned to death. Judges could be put to death too, if they accepted any bribes or special gifts, or showed favor to anyone appearing before them.

These laws may seem harsh to us today, but ancient historians agreed that Nezahualcóyotl was kind to the poor, to the sick, to widows and to the elderly. He spent much of his wealth on providing needy people with food and clothing, and he never stopped thinking about his people's well-being.

Bringing tribute

Poet and Statesman

I AM YOYONTZIN: I COME TO THIS PLACE

I am Yoyontzin. I come to this place
to gather the loveliest flowers
of friendship.
For a brief moment
my heart is joyful
here on earth.

I seek
the most beautiful songs.
I sing and dance for joy.
My heart brims with happiness.
I am Yoyontzin: I love
the most fragrant flowers
of friendship.

The kingdom of Tezcoco soon became a model of good government, virtue and culture for the ancient peoples of central Mexico's high plateau. Nezahualcóyotl founded a university, where the poets, priests, astronomers, philosophers, judges, historians and musicians gathered, each in their own academy. He also founded the royal library, where he collected and had copies made of all the codices, or books of manuscripts, that he could find. In Tezcoco people spoke a very refined Nahuatl, and the kingdom's sages and artists were known as the best in the region.

Nezahualcóyotl's royal palace was located on the eastern shore of Lake Tezcoco. The immense four-sided building, surrounded by vast walls, was half a mile square. It had more than three hundred rooms built around two main courtyards, and in each courtyard a ceremonial brazier burned day and night.

Besides his royal palace and gardens, Nezahualcóyotl had many parks, forests and hilly areas for hunting; orchards and fields for growing crops; bathing areas carved from the craggy rocks and country houses hewn from caverns.

But one place was his favorite of all. On Tezcotzinco, a wooded hill near the city, he constructed a magnificent villa with a high wall around it. He built an aqueduct to bring in water, and he also built canals, ponds and swimming pools, as well as paths, stairs and gardens. Nezahualcóyotl would go to his villa to rest, to meditate, or to delight in the company of his many concubines. The ancient tales that describe Tezcotzinco spare no words in their praise of its beauty. Nezahualcóyotl loved birds and had enormous birdcages built there for birds from all over Mesoamerica. He also planted many species of flowers, plants and trees from different regions. Some of them are still there today.

Nezahualcóyotl at Tezcotzinco

ONLY ONCE

Only once
do we live on earth.
Only what gives us joy
endures here.

Will the Place of Mystery
be like earth?
Will we have life there?
Will we know one another?

There is no sorrow there.
One remembers nothing.
Can that place be our home?
Will we live there as here?

LET US REVEL IN THE FLOWERS

Let us revel in the flowers
in our hands.
Let us wear around our necks
chains of fragrant blooms,
rainy-season flowers
opening their petal hearts.
Birds are singing
among the blossoms,
their feathers like the sun.

Only flowers
can cheer us,
only our songs
can banish gloom.
Fragrant petals
dispel bitterness.

The Giver of Life
invents them,
sends this rain of flowers,
the One who invents himself.
Lovely buds
dispel our grief.

I AM A POET

I am a poet, a bird
in the ring of flowering water,
I am a poet in the water's ring.
I am a reveler: my heart walks
on shore where people live,
raising my songs
to bring them joy.

But I am desolate.
Ah, my heart is desolate.
I am a poet on the shores
of the nine currents
of the Place of Mystery.

May they put me in my shroud
in the land of flowers!

I will go away. I will disappear.
They will put me on a bed
of yellow plumes,
and the crones will weep for me!

Tears shall wet my bones,
I shall descend to death
on the shadowy shore.

And when they lead me there,
my feathered robe
shall become smoke
upon the earth.

I will go away. I will disappear.
They will put me on a bed of yellow plumes.
The crones will weep for me.

THE ONE WHO INVENTS HIMSELF

*The house of the One who invents himself
is nowhere.
We look for him everywhere,
we invoke him everywhere.*

*He is the one who invents things
and he invents himself: God.*

*We seek him everywhere,
we yearn for his glory and his power.
But no one boasts
of being his friend.
He tires of us, misleads us:
only for a short time do we live near him.
He is no one's friend. We seek him in vain
while we live on earth.*

WE HAVE NO ROOTS

*We have no roots in the earth,
and nothing is real.
Only the One who rules the universe,
the God who gives life
is real.
Everything else is uncertain.
May our hearts not be tormented.
We have no roots.*

YOU PAINT THE WORLD WITH FLOWERS

*With flowers you paint the world,
Giver of Life,
with songs you color
all living things on earth.*

*Then you destroy them,
eagles or jaguars,
no matter how strong or brave.
With black ink you blot them out,
return them to the shadow.*

*I understand this secret:
the wise, the warriors, the princes,
we are all mortal.
Two by two, four by four,
all of us
will die.
We will all die on earth.*

*Like the plumy raiment
of the quetzal, the oriole,
the bluebird, we shall perish.*

*Meditate on this, my lords,
we shall disappear,
no one shall remain!*

The Heart of an Architect

I LISTEN TO A SONG

At last my heart is wise.
I listen to a song, gaze at a flower.
May their freshness
never fade!

Nezahualcóyotl had restored peace to his kingdom, created laws for his people and designed magnificent gardens and palaces. But now he found that even though he was surrounded by women, there was not a single one he wanted for his wife. And so he had no heir, because according to tradition an heir had to be a legitimate son. He was already forty years old. Who would inherit all the great things he had created? He became very sad.

One day Nezahualcóyotl was walking through the forest next to the lakeshore, overcome with sorrow. A poet named Cuacuauhtzin saw him there and took pity on him. He invited Nezahualcóyotl to come and eat at his palace. Cuacuauhtzin was soon going to marry an Aztec noblewoman named Azcalxochitzin, and to show Nezahualcóyotl honor, he ordered her to wait on him. Azcalxochitzin was so beautiful that "she took away all of the melancholy and sadness that Nezahualcóyotl had brought with him, and stole his heart," wrote the historian Fernando de Alva Ixtlilxóchitl, Nezahualcóyotl's descendant.

Azcalxochitzin waits on Nezahualcóyotl.

A few days later, Cuacuauhtzin received an order to join a war expedition against the kingdom of Tlaxcala. Two captains had been given royal orders to take him to the bloodiest place of combat and leave him there. Cuacuauhtzin realized this was a plot to kill him but, faithful to his king, he obeyed. Before he left, he wrote a poem, a sorrowful chant, that later became famous. As for Nezahualcóyotl, it is said that sending Cuacuauhtzin to perish in battle was the only evil deed he ever committed, and it tormented him for the rest of his life.

After Cuacuauhtzin died, Nezahualcóyotl came up with a complicated strategy to approach Azcalxochitzin without making her suspicious. He commanded that an enormous boulder be taken from a nearby village and placed in the woods on Tezcotzinco. Then he ordered many people to gather and watch as it was carried past, and he asked an elderly woman to tell Azcalxochitzin when to stand up to get a better look. When she did, he would gaze down on her from his platform and ask who she was. People would say she was the bride-to-be of the unfortunate Cuacuauhtzin, and that she had been left all alone. Then Nezahualcóyotl would ask that she be brought to his palace, saying it was not right for such a young and beautiful girl to live by herself.

So it was done, and soon after, Nezahualcóyotl announced that he would marry Azcalxochitzin. All the kings who were in alliances with him came to the wedding. The celebrations lasted four months, and people were still talking about them when the queen gave birth to the crown prince, Tetzauhpiltzintli.

Hardship, Misfortune and Conflict

WHERE CAN WE GO?

There is nowhere we can go
where death does not exist.
Shall this grieve us forever?
Let your heart understand it:
here, no one lives forever.
For even princes
are born to die.
Let your heart understand:
here, no one lives forever.

Throughout these years, as he built his palaces and got married, Nezahualcóyotl fought in many battles alongside his allies, especially the Aztecs. From 1435 to 1445, the armies of the kings of Tezcoco, Tenochtitlan and Tacuba fought together to conquer many lands. Izcóatl, the king of Tenochtitlan, died in 1440, and Moctezuma I, who was another of Nezahualcóyotl's uncles, took the throne. But even though Moctezuma and Nezahualcóyotl came from the same family and shared many of the same interests, they soon began to quarrel. Nezahualcóyotl objected to the bloodthirsty and warlike beliefs of the "people of the sun." He opposed the rite of human sacrifice, and argued about it many times with Moctezuma and his powerful adviser, Tlacaélel.

By now, the kingdom of Tezcoco had reached its greatest splendor. But hardship was soon to come. In 1445, a plague of locusts devoured the fields and the harvests, causing many people to go hungry. Then Nezahualcóyotl was drawn into a bloody war against the kingdom of Chalco, which lasted for more than twenty years.

In 1450, the valley of Mexico was struck by a snowfall so heavy that it destroyed houses, ruined forests and fields of crops, and set off an epidemic of colds that killed many people. Then there was a long drought that caused a famine, and the next year the famine got worse. In 1454, there was a total eclipse of the sun, which everyone believed would bring bad luck. The kings of Tezcoco, Tenochtitlan and Tacuba decided to stop collecting tribute for six years, and they distributed the corn stored in their granaries to help their people.

In Tezcoco, the temple priests began to put more and more pressure on Nezahualcóyotl. The gods were angry, they said, because he had opposed human sacrifice, and now they were punishing him. To appease the gods, the priests said that sacrifices had to be made and human hearts offered to the sun.

Saddened and alone in his beliefs, Nezahualcóyotl had to say yes. But he insisted that if captives were to be sacrificed, they must at least be men who were used to the idea of dying. They had to be soldiers.

And so began the "Flower Wars," a series of battles whose purpose was to provide sacrificial victims and whose name came from the many warriors who fell dead on the battlefield, like a rain of flowers.

Around the same time, Nezahualcóyotl accepted Moctezuma's invitation to plan and oversee construction of the Chapultepec aqueduct, to supply Tenochtitlan with drinking water. He did this even though he disagreed with the violent beliefs of the Aztec priests, which resembled those of the priests of Tezcoco. Moctezuma had already asked Nezahualcóyotl to build a dike to keep the city from flooding, and also to keep the water in Lake Tezcoco, which was salty,

from mixing with the fresh water from the nearby rivers.

But Nezahualcóyotl's misfortunes were not over. In 1464, his only son and heir, Tetzauhpiltzintli, was unjustly accused of plotting against him. Nezahualcóyotl's own code of justice decreed that this crime was punishable by death. At the trial, no one could prove that Prince Tetzauhpiltzintli was not guilty, and so he was executed.

Nezahualcóyotl loved his son very much, and cried bitterly at his death. The kingdom of Tezcoco was left with no one to succeed the king.

Child of the Sun and the Moon

WHO HAS SEEN GOD?

Alone, deep in the sky,
God is inventing words.
Who has seen him on the earth?
He is bored here, he grows vexed,
he is no one's friend.
Now I understand:
power and glory are naught.
Like gold and jade we shall descend
to the place of the dead.

Although Nezahualcóyotl could not stop the Aztecs from imposing their beliefs about how the universe was created, he himself avoided worshipping the official gods. Instead, he tried to understand life in a deeper, more meaningful way. He said he was the child of the sun and the moon, and he began to think that the gods who were worshipped in the temples were mere idols of stone. Maybe they were inert and lifeless, and could not speak or create anything. How could they have created the vast heavens, the sun, the moon, and the stars that lit the earth, or the rivers, the springs, the trees and the plants that grew there, or the people who lived there?

He gazed at the night sky and marveled at the immensity of the universe. Who could have created it all? It must have been a very powerful, mysterious and unknown god, and someday the people who lived here would believe him. He began to write his thoughts in beautiful poems, which also expressed his sadness that life is so short, and that we know so little about death and fear it so much.

Nezahualcóyotl called the unknown god Tloque Nahuaque, a name from the spiritual teachings of his Toltec ancestors. In his poems, he called this god "master of the close and near," "he who is invisible as night and intangible as the wind," "he who invents himself and invents life, who gives life to all," and "master of heaven, earth, and the land of the dead." To honor him, Nezahualcóyotl built a temple with a tall tower whose nine stories symbolized the nine levels or regions of heaven. The very top was consecrated to Tloque Nahuaque himself. It was decorated with an image of the night sky studded with stars, and was adorned with gold ornaments, gems and beautiful feathers, but with no figure or statue. Here Nezahualcóyotl would shut himself away for hours to pray and meditate in his search for truth.

With this in mind, and with great
sadness in my heart, I looked at
the heavens once again and began
to ponder the beauty of the sun,
the moon, the stars and all of
creation, and I said to myself that
our gods could not possibly have
created all of this grandeur, and
that the one who created it
was a very powerful god who
is hidden and known to no one.

Calamities and Wonders

MY FLOWERS WILL NOT PERISH

My flowers will not perish.
My songs will never cease.
I, the poet, raise them up.

Fragrant golden blooms,
they will scatter, they will spread.
But one day, nonetheless,
they will wither
and ascend to the heart of God.

The war against the kingdom of Chalco was growing more and more bitter. For twenty years, the armies of Tezcoco and Tenochtitlan had been trying in vain to conquer their enemy, but the battle-hardened Chalcas defended themselves fiercely and showed no mercy. No one could see a way out. Aging, overwhelmed by setbacks, with no heir and without hope that the queen would conceive another son, Nezahualcóyotl retreated once again to the woods of Tezcotzinco to seek inspiration.

There, the historians say, he fasted for forty days and forty nights, praising the invisible Tloque Nahuaque, the unknown god of the Toltecs, and beseeching the god to protect him and show him what to do.

One night after Nezahualcóyotl went back to his palace, he was meditating in his chamber when one of the guards heard someone call his name. Worried, the guard went out and found himself face to face with a mysterious messenger. "Have no fear," the stranger told him, "and tell the king that before noon tomorrow his army will win the war against the Chalcas, and the queen will bear a son who will succeed him."

When he heard this, Nezahualcóyotl thought the guard was making it up, and he commanded that he be punished. But the next day, the army of Tezcoco mounted a surprise attack on the Chalca king's camp. The attack was led by a young captain, barely eighteen years old, who had been born to Nezahualcóyotl out of wedlock and who wanted to show his courage. This time, the army of Tezcoco defeated the Chalcas once and for all.

On January 1, 1465, Queen Azcalxochitzin gave birth to a boy, who was named Nezahualpilli. Nezahualcóyotl could now be at peace, because he had a son to succeed him.

DO WE REALLY LIVE ON EARTH?

I, Nezahualcóyotl, ask,
do we really live on earth?
We shall not be here forever,
merely for an instant.
Jade may shatter,
gold may be destroyed,
quetzal plumes may tatter with the years.
We do not dwell forever on the earth,
merely for an instant.

Seven years later, when Nezahualcóyotl felt death approaching, he called for all his family, friends and members of his court, and told them:

"My children, family and subjects, no one knows better than you the grievous affronts inflicted upon us for many years by the leader of the province of Chalco and his people, and how, despite the many regions we were able to conquer, we could not defeat them, and how, counseled by the priests, and with great sadness and sorrow, I agreed to make human sacrifices… Now I am ready to die, and the comfort I take from this life is that, thanks to the almighty god who heard my prayers, I leave you with a king. And I am confident that he will govern in peace and tranquility, rewarding those who are worthy of it and punishing the unjust and the proud."

Nezahualcóyotl told his son, Prince Nezahualpilli, who was only seven years old, that he must not forget that his birth had been a miracle granted by the unknown god.

"Respect the god's temple," he told his son. "Make offerings but do not allow human sacrifices ever again, because this god rejects them and will severely punish anyone who performs them."

Then with tears in his eyes, Nezahualcóyotl bade farewell to his family, and asked them to leave his chamber. He told the servants guarding the door not to let anyone come in. A few hours later, he died. It was the morning of an unknown day in the year 1472. And so ended the life of Nezahualcóyotl, king of Tezcoco, the great ruler of ancient Mexico.

Epilogue

Like precious gems,
flowerbuds part
mid emerald leaves.
O princes,
we hold fragrant flowers
in our hands:
they are our jewels.
They are merely
loaned to us on earth.
Let us weave garlands
of perfumed flowers!
Fragrant flowers, O princes,
are our jewels.
They are merely
loaned to us on earth.

Nezahualpilli reigned for forty-four years, and under him Tezcoco became even more magnificent. Nezahualcóyotl's son was also a poet, architect, sorcerer, astronomer and a highly regarded astrologer. He died in 1515, four years before the Spanish came, and it is said he died of sorrow because he could foresee the end of his culture. All of the palaces, libraries, schools, temples, gardens and parks that Nezahualcóyotl had built and that Nezahualpilli expanded were destroyed during the Spanish conquest. All that we have left of these two great kings are memories, some archeological ruins and a handful of poems.

King Nezahualpilli

1402 Nezahualcóyotl is born in Tezcoco.

1408 He enters the *tlacateo*, a school for sons of the nobility.

1414 He takes the oath as crown prince of the kingdom of Tezcoco in a solemn ceremony.

1418 His father, Ixtlilxóchitl, is killed, and Nezahualcóyotl has to flee. He takes refuge in the court of Tenochtitlan.

1419 He hides in various places, fleeing from his enemies and fighting to get his kingdom back.

1420-26 He lives in Tenochtitlan, where he finishes his education and military training, and composes his first poems.

1427 After King Tezozómoc dies in Azcapotzalco, Maxtla takes the throne and repeatedly tries to kill Nezahualcóyotl. With the Triple Alliance of armies from Tezcoco, Tenochtitlan and Tacuba behind him, Nezahualcóyotl at last defeats Maxtla.

1430 He takes charge of various public works projects in Tenochtitlan, including the forest on Chapultepec hill.

1431 Nezahualcóyotl is declared king of Tezcoco.

1433-40 He begins to rebuild the kingdom of Tezcoco, constructing numerous palaces, temples, gardens, bathing areas and country homes. He founds the university, the library, the government councils and the courts.

1440 King Izcóatl of Tenochtitlan dies and is succeeded by Moctezuma I.

1443-44 Nezahualcóyotl completes the royal palace of Tezcoco and marries Azcalxochitzin.

1445 The Aztecs celebrate the "binding of the years" (the conclusion of the 52-year cycle in the Aztec solar calendar). Nezahualcóyotl's first son and heir to the throne is born. The war against the kingdom of Chalco begins and lasts twenty years.

1445-46 A plague of locusts attacks fields throughout the kingdom of Tezcoco, causing Nezahualcóyotl's subjects to go hungry.

1449 Invited by Moctezuma, Nezahualcóyotl plans and oversees construction of a dike to keep Tenochtitlan from flooding, and to keep the salt water in Lake Tezcoco from mixing with fresh water in the nearby rivers.

1450 The valley of Mexico is struck by a snowfall so heavy that it destroys many houses, forests and crops, and sets off a fatal epidemic of colds.

1451 The famine caused by a long drought gets worse.

1454 A total eclipse of the sun is seen as a terrible omen. The "Flower Wars" begin. Nezahualcóyotl plans and oversees construction of the Chapultepec aqueduct, which provides Tenochtitlan with drinking water.

1464 Tetzauhpiltzintli, who is Nezahualcóyotl's only legitimate son and heir to the throne, is accused of treason and executed.

1465 Nezahualcóyotl defeats the Chalcas once and for all. His second legitimate son, Nezahualpilli, is born.

1466 The Chapultepec aqueduct is completed.

1469 Moctezuma I dies.

1472 Nezahualcóyotl falls ill for the first time in his life, and dies in his palace in Tezcoco.

Aztecs: People belonging to the empire that ruled much of central and southern Mexico before the Spanish conquest in 1521.

Aztec calendar: The Aztecs used a solar calendar and a second calendar known as the sacred round. Every day had a name, a number and many meanings associated with it depending on where it fell in the combined calendar system.

codices: Plural form of codex, a book in manuscript form.

concubine: Woman who lives with a man to whom she is not married.

copal: Resin from tropical trees, which could be used for incense.

huéhuetl: Traditional wooden drum.

Nahuatl: Language spoken by the Aztecs and other native peoples of Mexico and Central America.

necromancy: Method of foretelling the future by calling on the spirits of the dead.

Tepanec: Mesoamerican people, with a culture related to that of the Aztecs, who arrived in the valley of Mexico in the late twelfth or early thirteenth century.

tlacateo: School for sons of the governing classes or the nobility.

tlatoani: Ruler.

Tloque Nahuaque: Name for the unknown god of the Toltecs.

Toltecs: Mesoamerican people who lived in central Mexico from the tenth to the thirteenth centuries, before the Aztecs.

For Further Reading

The Aztecs by Robert Hull. Austin: Raintree Steck-Vaughn Publishers, 1998.

The Aztec Empire by Nicholas Saunders and Tony Allan. Chicago: Heinemann Library, 2005.

Broken Shields by Claudia Burr, Krystyna Libura and Maria Cristina Urrutia. Toronto: Groundwood Books, 1997.

Hernando Cortés and the Conquest of Mexico by Gina De Angelis. Philadelphia: Chelsea House Publishers, 2000.

How to Be an Aztec Warrior by Fiona Macdonald. Washington, D.C.: National Geographic, 2005.

Lost Temple of the Aztecs by Shelley Tanaka, illustrations by Greg Ruhl. New York: Hyperion Books for Children/Madison Press Books, 1998.

The Sad Night: The Story of an Aztec Victory and a Spanish Loss by Sally Schofer Mathews. New York: Clarion Books, 1994.

Sun Stone Days/Tonaltin/Días de Piedra by Ianna Andréadis, with text by Elisa Amado, Sun Stone illustration by Felipe Dávalos. Toronto: Groundwood Books, 2007.

What the Aztecs Told Me by Krystyna Libura, Claudia Burr, Maria Cristina Urrutia. Toronto: Groundwood Books, 1997.

First published in Spanish as *El rey poeta: Biografía de Nezahualcóyotl* copyright © 2006
by CIDCLI; copyright © 2006 by Francisco Serrano
English translation and adaptation copyright © 2007 by Trudy Balch
Poetry translation copyright © 2007 by Jo Anne Engelbert
First English edition published in Canada and the USA by Groundwood Books in 2007

Groundwood Books / House of Anansi Press
110 Spadina Avenue, Suite 801, Toronto, Ontario M5V 2K4
Distributed in the USA by Publishers Group West
1700 Fourth Street, Berkeley, CA 94710

We acknowledge for their financial support of our publishing program the Government
of Canada through the Book Publishing Industry Development Program (BPIDP).

Library and Archives Canada Cataloging in Publication
Serrano, Francisco
The poet king of Tezcoco : a great leader of ancient Mexico / Francisco
Serrano ; illustrated by Pablo Serrano ; translated and adapted by Trudy Balch ; poetry
translated by Jo Anne Engelbert.
Translation of: El rey poeta : biografia de Nezahualcóyotl.
ISBN-13: 978-0-88899-787-6
ISBN-10: 0-88899-787-6
1. Nezahualcóyotl, King of Texcoco, 1402-1472–Juvenile literature. 2. Tezcucan
Indians–Kings and rulers–Biography–Juvenile literature. 3. Mexico–History–To
1519–Juvenile literature. 4. Indian poetry–Mexico–Translations into English.
I. Serrano, Pablo II. Balch, Trudy III. Engelbert, Jo Anne IV. Title.
F1219.75.N49S47 2007   j972'.018092   C2006-905605-6

Designed by Rogelio Rangel
Printed and bound in China

This map shows the valley of Mexico in the 1400s. The poet king Nezahualcóyotl ruled the kingdom of Tezcoco, which lay to the east of a vast lake that was also called Tezcoco. In 1521, Spaniard Hernan Cortés established Mexico City on the ruins of Tenochtitlan and Tlatelolco. Today the lake has disappeared and Mexico City is one of the biggest cities in the world, covering the area shown on this map and much more.